ARIZONA

by Jonatha A. Brown

GARETH**STEVENS**
GS
PUBLISHING
A Member of the WRC Media Family of Companies

Please visit our web site at: www.garethstevens.com
For a free color catalog describing Gareth Stevens Publishing's
list of high-quality books and multimedia programs, call
1-800-542-2595 (USA) or 1-800-387-3178 (Canada).
Gareth Stevens Publishing's fax: (414) 332-3567.

Library of Congress Cataloging-in-Publication Data

Brown, Jonatha A.
    Arizona / Jonatha A. Brown.
      p. cm. — (Portraits of the states)
    Includes bibliographical references and index.
    ISBN 0-8368-4660-5 (lib. bdg.)
    ISBN 0-8368-4679-6 (softcover)
    1. Arizona—Juvenile literature. I. Title. II. Series.
F811.3.B756   2006
979.1—dc22   2005044482

This edition first published in 2006 by
Gareth Stevens Publishing
A Member of the WRC Media Family of Companies
330 West Olive Street, Suite 100
Milwaukee, WI 53212 USA

This edition copyright © 2006 by Gareth Stevens, Inc.

Editorial direction: Mark J. Sachner
Project manager: Jonatha A. Brown
Editor: Catherine Gardner
Art direction and design: Tammy West
Picture research: Diane Laska-Swanke
Production: Jessica Morris and Robert Kraus

Picture credits: Cover, p. 10 © Eugene G. Schulz; pp. 4, 26, 27 © Bernadette
Heath; pp. 5, 6 © Corel; p. 8 © PhotoDisc; p. 9 © ArtToday; p. 15 © CORBIS;
pp. 16, 29 © Kerrick James.com; pp. 20, 22, 24 © Gibson Stock Photography;
p. 25 © Robyn Beck/AFP/Getty Images; p. 28 © Mike Nelson/AFP/Getty Images

Printed in the United States of America

1 2 3 4 5 6 7 8 9 10 09 08 07 06

CONTENTS

Words that are defined in the Glossary appear
in **bold** the first time they are used in the text.

On the Cover: The Saguaro cactus grows only in the Sonoran Desert.
It can grow up to 50 feet (15 meters) high.

Introduction

When you think of Arizona, what comes to mind? The Grand Canyon? A tall cactus rising up from a dry, brown desert? Arizona is known for these things. Yet the state also has high mountains that are often capped with snow. It has sparkling lakes, too. Arizona is a land of contrasts.

This state is home to many Mexican Americans. They enrich Arizona with their language and festivals. Native Americans live there, too. Some still practice old ways of weaving cloth and raising crops.

Welcome to Arizona! It is a great state to explore.

The Grand Canyon is one of the greatest natural wonders in North America. Some parts of the canyon are more than 1 mile (1.6 kilometers) deep.

The state flag of Arizona.

ARIZONA FACTS

- Became the 48th U.S. State: February 14, 1912
- Population (2004): 5,743,834
- Capital: Phoenix
- Biggest Cities: Phoenix, Tucson, Mesa, Glendale
- Size: 113,635 square miles (294,315 square kilometers)
- Nickname: The Grand Canyon State
- State Tree: Palo verde
- State Flower: Blossom of the saguaro cactus
- State Mammal: Ringtailed cat
- State Bird: Cactus wren

History

Arizona is in a part of the country that is known as the American Southwest. Native Americans first came to this area about twelve thousand years ago. These people moved from place to place. They hunted animals and gathered wild plants to eat. Much later, Natives began farming. Some groups of Natives dug trenches to bring water to their fields. Some wove cloth and made pottery.

By the late 1400s, more Natives had come to this land. They were members of the Apache and Navajo tribes. These people were more warlike. They defeated some of the more peaceful tribes.

Long ago, some Natives built villages in the walls of cliffs. These ruins are now part of the Montezuma Castle National Monument.

Early Settlers

By the early 1500s, Spain had begun taking land from Native people in Mexico. Soon, the Spanish began to take land in the Southwest, too. In 1539, Fray Marcos de Niza explored the area. He was a Spaniard who had started his trip in Mexico.

Spanish priests came north from Mexico in the late 1600s. They set up churches called missions in southern Arizona. Many Natives did not want the white explorers and priests to settle there. They raided the missions and tried to drive the white settlers out. The Spanish reacted by building sturdy forts.

In 1821, Mexico broke away from Spain. Soon after, Spain gave up its claim to the American Southwest. Much of the area became a **territory** of Mexico in 1824.

At this time, most of the people who lived in Arizona were Natives. Only a few white people lived there. White trappers and traders, however, soon moved in.

IN ARIZONA'S HISTORY

Looking for Gold

When de Niza was in Mexico, he heard that there was gold in the lands to the north. He came to Arizona hoping to find great riches. When he did not find gold, he left. Other Spanish explorers followed, but they did not find gold either.

7

The Spanish built the San Xavier Mission near what is now Tucson. The mission church is often called the "White Dove of the Desert."

Most of them were from the United States.

In 1846, Mexico and the United States went to war. They were fighting for control of the Southwest. This war lasted for two years. When Mexico lost, it gave up a large amount of land. A few years later,

IN ARIZONA'S HISTORY

A Final Fight for Freedom

Reservations were terrible places to live in the 1800s. The land was nearly useless. The Natives had very difficult lives. In 1885, Chief Geronimo led a group of Apaches away from their reservation. The Army chased them and tried to make them return. Geronimo and his men fought for their freedom for more than a year. In the end, however, the Army won. This time, the Army forced the Apaches to move all the way to Oklahoma.

the United States bought the rest of the land in Arizona from Mexico.

In 1863, the Arizona Territory was formed. More settlers arrived in the area. At first, the Natives were willing to share the land with them. But the settlers did not want to share the land. They wanted to own it.

The U.S. government supported the settlers. The nation's leaders did not have respect for Native ways. U.S. leaders made promises to the Natives and then broke them. Finally, a war began in the early 1860s.

FACTS

Phoenix

In 1867, a tiny town sprung up in the Arizona desert. Many years passed before the town had a name that stuck. Finally, the town leaders settled on the name Phoenix. A phoenix is a **mythical** bird. According to legend, this bird burns up and then rises again from its own ashes. The city of Phoenix was a little like that bird. It rose over the remains of an ancient Native settlement.

The Navajo people fought the U.S. Army for two years. The Apache people fought for much longer. The last

Geronimo was captured by the U.S. cavalry in 1886. He escaped from these men two days later.

9

Natives were beaten in 1872. They were forced to move to reservations.

The Theodore Roosevelt Dam was built across the Salt River in the early 1900s.

Growth

In the late 1800s, Arizona changed a lot. Farmers began **irrigating** more and more land. Once they could bring water to their fields, they could grow more crops. Cattle and sheep ranching grew, too. Railroads were built. They connected the territory to other parts of the country. At about the same time, gold and silver were found near Tombstone. Copper mines opened, too. Many people came to work in the mines.

Arizona became a state in 1912. George W. P. Hunt was the first governor. Hunt worked hard to improve life in Arizona. When he was in office, dams were built and irrigation canals were dug. These improvements helped

FUN FACTS

The Secret Code of the Navajo

People of the Navajo tribe speak their own language. This language is hard to learn. During World War II, the U.S. Marines wanted to send secret messages. They did not want the enemy to listen to the messages and learn their plans. About four hundred Navajos agreed to help the Marines. They invented a code based on their language. They used the code to send messages. The trick worked, and the enemy never figured out the code. Thanks to these Navajo heroes, the Marines' plans remained a secret.

farmers raise more crops. They also helped towns and cities grow. During this time, mining and **tourism** did well, too.

World Wars

World War I began in 1914. Many companies came to the state to make goods for the war. During the war, Arizona cotton, copper, and beef were in great demand.

After the war, the U.S. Army did not need as much copper. The price of copper fell. Mines in Arizona closed, and many miners were out of work. By the 1930s, most of the nation's businesses were in trouble. This period was called the Great Depression. Many

IN ARIZONA'S HISTORY

Changing an Unfair Law

For many years, the state law said that Native people could not vote. After World War II ended, the state Supreme Court said this law was unfair. It said the law must be changed. Native Americans finally got the right to vote in 1948.

factories closed. Farmers went out of business. Arizona was as poor as the rest of the nation. Even so, many people moved to the state during this time.

World War II brought jobs back to the state in the early 1940s. The U.S. Air Force set up bases in Arizona. The state's farms and factories made goods to help fight the war.

Recent Changes

After the war, the state kept growing. It began to use up its supplies of underground water. The leaders of the state had to figure out how to get more water to the cities. In the late 1900s, they hired people to build pipelines and canals. These pipes and canals now carry water from the Colorado River to other parts of the state. This water allows

Famous People of Arizona

César Chávez

Born: March 31, 1927, Yuma, Arizona

Died: April 23, 1993, San Luis, Arizona

César Chávez was a Mexican American who helped farm workers all over the United States. For many years, these people worked in terrible conditions for very low pay. If they complained, they were often fired. Chávez helped the field workers form a **labor union**. Then, they worked together to change their lives. With Chávez in the lead, they refused to work until farmers treated them fairly. After a long struggle, the farmers gave in to some of the demands. Chávez became a hero to people who worked in the fields.

millions of people to enjoy living in Arizona.

1539	Fray Marcos de Niza explores parts of what is now Arizona.
1752	Tubac becomes the first European settlement in Arizona.
1824	Mexico takes control of the area from Spain.
1848	The United States gains control of most of Arizona.
1854	The United States buys the rest of the land that is now Arizona.
1877	The first railroad comes to Arizona; silver is discovered near Tombstone.
1886	Geronimo and other Apaches surrender to the U.S. Army.
1889	Phoenix becomes the capital of Arizona.
1912	Arizona becomes the forty-eighth U.S. state.
1948	Native Americans are granted the right to vote.
1968	Work begins on a project to bring water from the Colorado River to big cities in Arizona.
1998	Women are elected governor, attorney general, and secretary of state in Arizona.
2001	The Arizona Diamondbacks win the World Series in baseball.

People

Arizona covers a lot of land. In fact, it is the sixth largest state in the nation. Yet, this large state does not have a large **population**. Fewer than six million people live in Arizona.

About three-fourths of the people live in or near Phoenix. Phoenix is the largest city in the state and the sixth largest city in the nation. Tucson is the state's next largest city. Other large cities in the state are Mesa and Glendale.

Hispanics: In the 2000 U.S. Census, 25.3 percent of the people in Arizona called themselves Latino or Hispanic. Most of them or their relatives came from places where Spanish is spoken. They may come from different racial backgrounds.

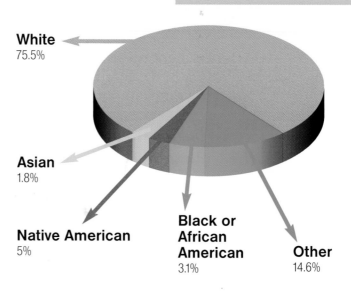

The People of Arizona

Total Population 5,743,834

White
75.5%

Asian
1.8%

Native American
5%

Black or African American
3.1%

Other
14.6%

Percentages are based on the 2000 Census.

A Mix of People

Arizona has a large Native population. These Natives belong to more than twenty tribes. The Navajo tribe is the largest. Many Navajo people still speak their own language. Natives own more than one-fourth of the land in the state. Most of this land is on reservations.

Hispanic, or **Latino**, people have been moving

to Arizona for hundreds of years. Most of them have come from Mexico. Some have come from other Latin American countries. Today, more than one-fourth of the population of the state is Hispanic. Some of these people speak both English and Spanish. Others speak

These children go to school at St. John's Mission. They are happy to be outdoors during recess.

of the early white settlers came from Texas and other southern states. Later, more white people came from Europe. Many came from Ireland and Britain.

Growing Fast

Today, Arizona is growing much faster than most other states. Thousands of people move to the state every year. Many of them are older men and women who have retired from their jobs in colder parts of the country. They have come to enjoy the sun and warm weather.

only Spanish. In many parts of Arizona, signs are written in both languages.

As in most U.S. states, most of the people who live in Arizona are white. Many

People move to Arizona from other countries, too.

More than half of the recent **immigrants** came from Mexico. Other immigrants are from China, India, and other parts of the world.

Education and Religion

Tucson was the first city in the state to have a public school. This school opened in 1871. Fourteen years later, the first university was founded in Tucson. It was the University of Arizona. That same year, a teaching college opened in Tempe. It has since become Arizona State University.

Most people in the state are Christian. About one in five of these people is Catholic. Most of the other Christians are Protestants. Almost 6 percent of the people practice Native American religions. Jews, Buddhists, and Muslims live in Arizona, too.

Famous People of Arizona

Cochise

Born: about 1815, Chiricahua Territory, northern Mexico

Died: June 8, 1874, new Chiricahua Reservation, Arizona

Cochise was an Apache chief. He and his people lived at peace with the whites for many years. Then, Cochise was **accused of** kidnapping a white child. He was innocent, but the whites thought he was guilty. They shot Cochise three times when they captured him. He was hurt, but he still managed to escape. Cochise hid in the Chiricahua Mountains for the next ten years. He left his stronghold only to raid white settlements. In 1872, he gave up and was sent to live in a reservation. He lived there for the rest of his life.

The Land

Arizona has three main regions. The Colorado **Plateau** covers the northern part of the state. The Sonoran Desert lies in the south. The Transition Zone is in the middle.

The Colorado Plateau

The Colorado Plateau is made up of high, fairly flat land. In many places, this land has been deeply cut by canyons and valleys. A very famous canyon is the Grand Canyon. It is about 1 mile (1.6 km) deep. People standing on the rim can see the Colorado River sparkling far below.

Near Flagstaff, the San Francisco Mountains jut up from the plateau. Humphrey's Peak, the highest peak in the state, is found there. It is 12,633 feet (3,851 m) high.

The Mogollon (MUG ee un) Rim forms the southern edge of the plateau. It is a high stretch of land that drops off steeply to the south.

The Colorado Plateau is the wettest, coolest part of Arizona. During the

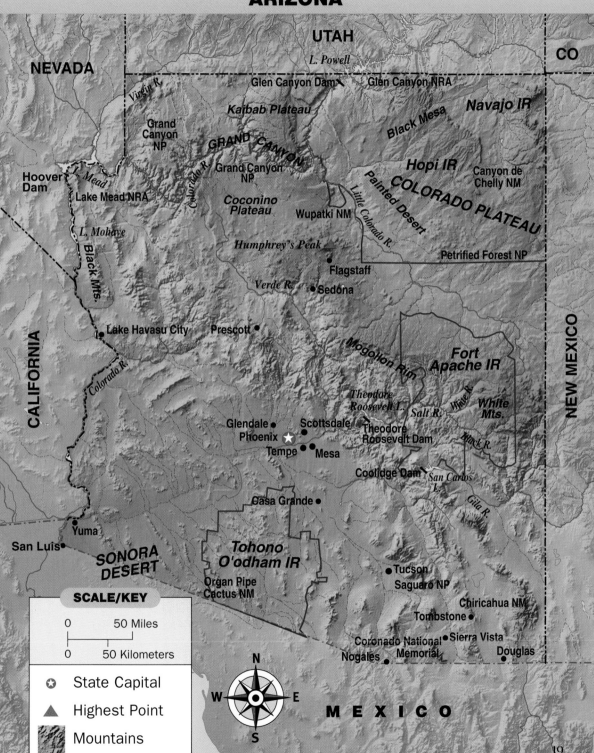

ARIZONA

UTAH

NEVADA

CO

L. Powell

Glen Canyon Dam   Glen Canyon NRA

Virgin R.

Kaibab Plateau   Black Mesa   Navajo IR

Grand
Canyon
NP   GRAND CANYON

Hoover
Dam   L. Mead   Hopi IR   Canyon de
Chelly NM

Lake Mead NRA   Grand Canyon
NP   COLORADO PLATEAU

Colorado R.

Coconino
Plateau   Wupatki NM   Painted Desert

L. Mohave   Little Colorado R.

Humphrey's Peak   Petrified Forest NP

Black Mts.   Flagstaff

Verde R.   Sedona

CALIFORNIA

Lake Havasu City   Prescott

Mogollon Rim   Fort
Apache IR

Colorado R.   Theodore
Roosevelt L.   Verde R.   White
Mts.

Salt R.

Glendale   Scottsdale   Theodore
Roosevelt Dam   Black R.

Phoenix

Tempe   Mesa

Coolidge Dam   San Carlos
L.

Casa Grande   Gila R.

NEW MEXICO

Yuma

San Luis

SONORA
DESERT   Tohono
O'odham IR

Organ Pipe
Cactus NM   Tucson

Saguaro NP

Chiricahua NM

Tombstone

Coronado National
Memorial   Sierra Vista

Nogales   Douglas

M E X I C O

SCALE/KEY

0   50 Miles

0   50 Kilometers

N
W   E
S

⊗ State Capital

▲ Highest Point

Mountains

19

winter, snow and freezing temperatures are common in the mountains.

Pine and fir trees grow in the mountains and on the Mogollon Rim. Bear and bighorn sheep can be found there. Other parts of the plateau have small, scrubby trees, such as junipers and piñon pines. Rabbits and

Major Rivers

Colorado River
1,450 miles (2,350 km) long

Gila River
500 miles (805 km) long

Little Colorado River
315 miles (507 km) long

pronghorn antelope live in these areas.

The Transition Zone

The Transition Zone starts just south of the Mogollon Rim. In this area, the land is about 2,000 feet (600 m) lower than it is on the Rim. Mountain ranges cover this part of the state. The White

Monument Valley is known for its red spires and rocky peaks. Many Western movies have been filmed there.

FACTS

Rivers and Lakes

Arizona is crisscrossed by rivers. The Colorado River is the largest. It runs along the state's western border. This river provides water to much of the state. Many streambeds in Arizona are dry most of the year. Water runs through them only after a heavy rain.

Dams have been built across most of the state's rivers. Lakes have formed behind the dams. In many places, the dry, brown desert comes right down to the edge of a beautiful man-made lake! Lake Powell is the largest of the state's man-made lakes. It was formed by damming the Colorado River.

Mountains are especially pretty. They are covered with pine trees and lovely, green meadows. Small natural lakes can be found in some of the meadows.

The Sonoran Desert

A desert covers the southern part of the state. It is made up of low-lying land that is dotted with mountains. The biggest cities in the state are found in this area.

In the Sonoran Desert, the summers are very hot and winters are mild. Little rain falls in the desert. Even so, plants such as cactus and **agave** are common. Mesquite and palo verde trees thrive, too. The palo verde is the state tree. Like many desert plants, it has sharp spines.

Lizards, snakes, **javelinas**, and coyotes are some desert animals. Ground squirrels and cottontails are common. Doves, cactus wrens, and quail nest in the trees and cactuses and on the ground.

Economy

In Arizona, more people have service jobs than any other kind of work. Service workers help other people. Doctors and nurses have service jobs. Teachers and waiters have service jobs, too. Some service workers help tourists. During winter, Arizona's warm weather draws tourists from colder places. These visitors eat in restaurants. They stay in hotels. They go to special events and visit museums. Tourism means jobs for many workers in Arizona.

Many people who live in Arizona work in factories. Some factories make parts for computers, airplanes, and other machines. Guided missiles, helicopters, and spacecraft are also built in this state.

Farming is still important in Arizona. Here, melon plants are growing in an irrigated field.

Ranching, Farming, and Mining

Ranches and farms cover about half of Arizona's land. The main farm product in the state is beef. Sheep are raised, too. Irrigation makes it possible to grow many crops. Cotton is the top crop. Some farmers grow lettuce and other vegetables. **Citrus fruits** also are widely grown. Other farm products in the state are grains, such as corn, wheat, and barley.

Arizona leads the nation in copper production. Silver and gold are mined as well. Turquoise is found in the state. It is Arizona's state gemstone. Crushed stone and gravel are two other important products that come from the earth in this state.

How Money Is Made in Arizona

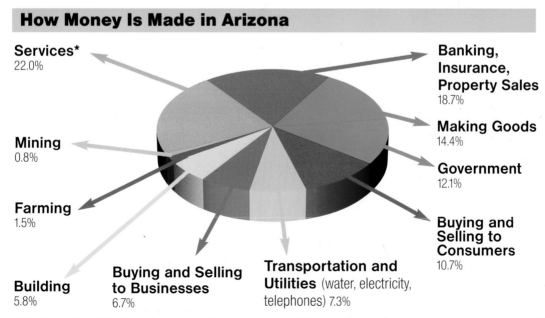

Services* 22.0%

Banking, Insurance, Property Sales 18.7%

Making Goods 14.4%

Mining 0.8%

Government 12.1%

Farming 1.5%

Buying and Selling to Consumers 10.7%

Building 5.8%

Buying and Selling to Businesses 6.7%

Transportation and Utilities (water, electricity, telephones) 7.3%

* Services include jobs in hotels, restaurants, auto repair, medicine, teaching, and entertainment.

Government

Phoenix is the capital of Arizona. The state's leaders work in this city. The state government has three parts. They are the executive, legislative, and judicial branches.

Executive Branch

The executive branch carries out the state's laws. The governor is the leader of this branch. A team of people called the **cabinet** works for the governor.

Legislative Branch

The Arizona legislature has two parts. They are the Senate and the House of

The leaders of the state work in the capitol building in Phoenix.

John McCain is a U.S. senator from Arizona. He thinks for himself and his ideas sometimes surprise people.

Representatives. These two groups work together to make laws for the state.

Judicial Branch

Judges and courts make up the judicial branch. Judges and courts may decide whether people who have been accused of committing crimes are guilty.

Local Government

Arizona has fifteen counties. Each county is led by a team of three people. Cities are run by a city council and a city manager or mayor.

Navajo Nation

The Navajo Nation owns a large area of land. Part of this land is in Arizona. The rest is in New Mexico and Utah. The Navajo Nation is run by a tribal government. The tribal leaders meet in Window Rock.

ARIZONA'S STATE GOVERNMENT

Executive		Legislative		Judicial	
Office	**Length of Term**	**Body**	**Length of Term**	**Court**	**Length of Term**
Governor	4 years	Senate		Supreme (5 justices)	6 years
Secretary of State	4 Years	(30 members)	2 years	Appeals (21 judges)	6 years
		House of Representatives			
		(60 members)	2 years		

Things to See and Do

Cowboy Town

Going to Tombstone is like taking a trip back in time! Many old-style buildings line the streets. Tourists and local people dress the way people did in the Old West. Visitors stroll down the streets and stop by the OK Corral. They watch actors pretend to fight a gun battle that took place there in 1881.

If you want to see what life was like in the Old West, be sure to visit Tombstone.

The Grand Canyon is one of the most popular tourist spots in the world. But it is only one of many natural wonders in Arizona. Meteor Crater is a huge hole in the ground. It was formed when a **meteorite** struck Earth long ago. Oak Creek Canyon is a great spot to hike. Sedona is known for its red rocks and cliffs. National parks and forests can be found all over Arizona, too.

Museums

Tucson has many museums. The Pima Air and Space Museum is well

This woman is weaving a basket by hand. She is one of many Natives who still follow the old ways.

Famous People of Arizona

Sandra Day O'Connor

Born: March 26, 1930, El Paso, Texas

Sandra Day O'Connor was raised in Arizona. She grew up on a cattle ranch. She became a lawyer and then a judge. In 1981, O'Connor became the first woman to serve on the U.S. Supreme Court. In 2005, she decided to leave the Court. She has written a book about growing up in Arizona. It is *Lazy B: Growing up on a Cattle Ranch in the American Southwest*.

known. Visitors who like old airplanes should be sure to see it. Another museum shows the ways animals and plants live in the desert. Still other museums show what life was like in Arizona many years ago.

The Heard Museum is in Phoenix. It has displays of Native American art. The Pueblo Grande Museum is not far away. Here, visitors can see how Native people once lived.

Sports

For baseball fans, Arizona is a dream come true! Many major league teams hold

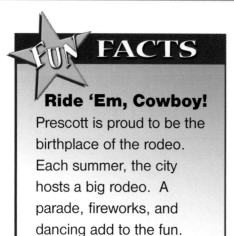

FUN FACTS

Ride 'Em, Cowboy!

Prescott is proud to be the birthplace of the rodeo. Each summer, the city hosts a big rodeo. A parade, fireworks, and dancing add to the fun.

2001: Luis Gonzalez brings in the winning run for the Diamondbacks during the last game of the World Series!

spring training in the state. During the regular season, the Arizona Diamondbacks draw big crowds to their home games in Phoenix. The "D-Backs" won the World Series in 2001.

Phoenix has more big-league teams. The Phoenix Coyotes play hockey. The Suns are a basketball team. Football fans cheer for the Arizona Cardinals.

In summer, many people head for the lakes and rivers. They go boating, ride jet skis, and swim.

Fairs and Festivals

People in Arizona celebrate Cinco de Mayo. This is a Mexican American festival. Each year on May 5, young and old turn out for a

Famous People of Arizona

George Crook

Born: September 8, 1830, near Dayton, Ohio

Died: March 21, 1890, Chicago, Illinois

In the 1870s, General George Crook came to Arizona. His job was to end the fighting between Apaches and whites. Unlike most whites, he treated Native people fairly. He kept his promises. Crook earned the respect of many Natives and helped bring peace. Late in his life, he spoke out against the way the U.S. government treated Native people.

Dancers put on a colorful show during a Mexican American festival in Tumacacori.

good time. They listen to music, eat, and celebrate Mexican American culture.

The Navajo Nation holds a fair in September. Visitors learn about Navajo culture. They listen to music and watch dances. They try Native foods, such as fry bread. This treat is a big round of fried dough that is covered with a sweet topping.

GLOSSARY

accused of — blamed for

agave — a desert plant that has sword-shaped leaves with sharp spines

cabinet — a group of advisors to a leader

citrus fruits — oranges, grapefruits, limes, lemons, and other similar fruits

Hispanic or Latino — coming from a Spanish-speaking background

immigrants — people who leave one country to live in another country

irrigating — bringing water to fields through pipes, ditches, and canals

javelinas — wild pigs

labor union — a group of workers that tries to get better pay and conditions for its members

meteorite — a chunk of rock from outer space that has landed on Earth

mythical — imaginary

petrified — changed to stone

plateau — a large area of flat land that is higher than the land around it

population — the number of people who live in a place, such as a state

reservations — areas of land set aside by the government for a special purpose, such as land set aside for use by a group of Native Americans

territory — an area of land that belongs to a country

tourism — traveling for pleasure

Books

And It Is Still That Way: Legends Told by Arizona Indian Children. Byrd Baylor. (Cinco Puntos Press)

Arizona. Rookie Read-About Geography (series). Michelle Aki Becker. (Children's Press)

Geronimo. History Maker Bios (series). Catherine A. Welch. (Lerner)

Grand Canyon. Linda Vieira (Walker Books for Young Readers)

Life in a Hopi Village. Picture the Past (series). Sally Senzel Isaacs. (Heinemann Library)

This Place Is Dry: Arizona's Sonoran Desert. Imagine Living Here (series). Vicki Cobb. (Walker Books for Young Readers)

Web Sites

Arizona Sonora Desert Museum: Especially for Kids
www.desertmuseum.org/kids/

Enchanted Learning: Arizona
www.enchantedlearning.com/usa/states/arizona/

Ghost Towns of Arizona
www.ghosttowns.com/states/az/az.html

A Pima Remembers
www.uapress.arizona.edu/samples/sam504.htm

INDEX